Beyond
MANAGEMENT
BY
OBJECTIVES

J. D. Batten

A DIVISION OF
AMERICAN MANAGEMENT ASSOCIATIONS

Library of Congress catalog card number: 66-29660
ISBN 0-8144-5614-6

Contents

Contents

Preface to the Reissued Edition

S o much has happened since the original edition of this book was published: the concept of "future shock" was developed; the Vietnam trauma moved onto center stage and exited; and inflation, the activities of the OPEC nations, the Arab-Israeli problems, and the ebb and flow of domestic crises have brought about a world of change, heightened needs, and, above all, *opportunities.*

At the center of it all is the manager, the leader (I use the terms interchangeably). For decades, perhaps centuries, the true role of the manager was not clearly perceived, even though in Jethro's advice to Moses in the Old Testament the need for effective organization was clearly spelled out. Somehow, a great distinction between the leader and the manager evolved. The "leader" was thought to be a charismatic creature and the "manager" was perceived as an overseer and manipulator of details. Of course, neither representation was entirely correct.

At last we are understanding that the manager is the person who *makes things happen* in such diverse areas as science, education, agriculture, government, religion, business, and every other phase of human endeavor where achievement depends on effective group effort. I predict that the development of management tools and managerial skills will ultimately be given more emphasis and represent a greater investment than any other area of practice employed by modern man. It is for these reasons that I present this book. It is designed not only to proffer some answers, tools, techniques, and "how-to" advice, but also to stimulate *questions* and to foster a restless, questing *attitude*.

Modern managers and the managers of tomorrow are not pushers or directors, but rather leaders. They recognize the ineffectiveness of methods that push, compress, repress, depress, and rigidify. They are committed to leading, evoking, scheduling, and monitoring within a *systematic* framework. It is crucial that they become experts in clarifying, defining, and systematically accomplishing expectations. At the heart of all truly effective systems of management are clear, logical, and thoroughly communicated expectations. The managers who understand motivation know that motive is just another word for expectation and that:

- Motive is the root word in motivation.
- Skillfully instrumented motivation has a profound impact on the bottom line.

It is my hope that readers will find here useful insights and stimulation, not only in how to manage by objectives but also in how to broaden and enrich their managerial and personal lifestyles.

Joe D. Batten

Introduction

In larger books I have set forth the broad and definitive philosophy of tough-minded management. But busy executives — many of whom have provided invaluable feedback — want *meat*. They want "how to"; they want *system* at the overall corporate design level — with no frills.

So I have boiled down, distilled, and updated my own and my colleagues' recent thinking and experience to produce a digested scheme of, and design for, dynamic management. Here is an approach that is equally applicable to manufacturing, processing, retailing, or any other company endeavor.

I feel deeply that establishing goals and objectives is not enough for the company which is dedicated to excellence. The real stuff of the organization, the human minds without which there is no organization, must be integrated with the other resources: the money, materials, time, and space available to the business. Individualism is vital, but a combination of individuals will be only a group of individuals — not an organization —

unless the requirements for successful operation are skillfully blended to insure that two plus two equals five — or more. Involvement and conviction must precede meaningful commitment.

To stop at a given point and say, "We now have management by objectives," is a source of potential business mediocrity. It can become a crutch simply because it produces complacency while managers and supervisors sit back and wait for great things to happen. The statement of objectives is, at most, about 30 percent of the management job. It is only the bones, the skeleton of the corporate body. The problem is to move out beyond management by objectives and begin the process of making the organization operative through a planned motivational climate.

SECTION ONE

Motivation

Throughout the length and breadth of our country big jobs are going unfilled. Why? Because there is a real shortage of big men. I mean men with punch, force, vision, imagination, and guts. It has become almost a truism to say that successful business management depends on the caliber of the people in the business. All thoughtful managers and students of management soon discover this. They realize that a beautiful plant full of impressive equipment is useless unless someone turns on the electric current and pulls the switches on the machines.

People make the whole difference, I say. And this is true. But the mere presence of a skillfully recruited group of people still insures nothing but activity, directed or misdirected. What does it take to get results? A "program"? A "procedure"? A new "technique"? These have their place, but complete reliance on tools, techniques, and programs simply has not met the test so far. Industrial psychologists tell us that the average person seldom ever exceeds 20 percent of his potential for productivity. What is lacking? Motivation!

WHAT IS MOTIVATION?

Nine-tenths of an iceberg, they tell us, is below the surface of the water — out of sight. So it is with motivation. A small part of it is seen and understood; but since the rest is not readily visible, it is largely ignored.

Scarcely a management clinic or seminar is held where motivation is not discussed. But how many understand it? How many, in particular, sense its full impact on productivity and profit? Motivation literally means "action to achieve motive." Business is currently spending large sums on the "action" but very little on the "motive."

The following analogy illustrates why motivation is so important. Some components of a semi-automatic turret lathe include:

- Nuts.
- Bolts.
- Dials.
- Gauges.
- Metal.
- Gears.

These are useless until they are assembled and the lathe is put to work. Similarly, some attributes of a person include:

- Interests.

- Aptitudes.
- Temperament.
- Hopes.
- Fears.
- Blood.
- Bones.
- Flesh.

These are meaningless until the man or woman possessing them is motivated.

Thus resources and combinations of resources — whether men, money, materials, time, or space — are meaningless until motivation takes place. Motivation is the vital, central mainstream of all worthwhile living. Without motivation, we have no motives and no actions; we function like bland, tepid human vegetables. In contrast, when we have strong motives and strong actions, and when these are positively directed and purposefully carried through, we experience abundant living — mentally, spiritually, physically, and materially.

FALSE STARTS AND ASSUMPTIONS

Certainly we may logically wonder why a definitive, logical, and workable approach to motivation has not been developed by managers to a level resembling the optimum. There are a number of reasons.

First of all, management has attempted to meet the challenge of motivation with programs, tools, and techniques. Efforts have been based on a superficial application of the psychological theories of academicians rather than the application of those principles which can be developed only in the ever-constant kaleidoscope of actual business problem solving. Practices have too often been based on the premise that employees —

1. Do not want to work.
2. Have no capacity for planning.
3. Are entitled to only a sort of second-class dignity.
4. Are entirely self-seeking.

It has frequently been presumed that the very nature of business makes it impossible to eliminate internal politics, friction, and emotional turmoil. Then, too, management has not provided sufficient goals, objectives, or targets. Thus most subordinate executives have no real idea why they are working or why they should improve the status quo — unless it is pure self-aggrandizement. In few instances has top management succeeded in making the team feel like star performers in a stimulating, pulse-quickening drama of private enterprise. Rather, the process of getting the day over with is usually paramount.

Top management has spent little time or effort in learning about the potential of positive thinking and living and applying it to the business scene. Many feel this is the type of thing their subordinates could profit from — it shouldn't concern anyone who "has it made." For this very reason we see deep-seated negativism in the lower echelons of management — fears and apprehensions that approach the abnormal. No amount of individual effort to grow and develop positively will be completely successful if the motivational climate is negative and hostile and if other members of the group are apathetic or running scared. Positiveness must flow down from the top.

The general, specific, and intermediate results required of each member of the management team are scarcely understood. Most job descriptions, for instance, have been a series of tepid, generalized statements of responsibility only. Clear, unambiguous results requirements have seldom been developed.

Internal communications have often been clogged and choked by terminology and practices that have grown up because company management wallows in a morass of "nice-guyism," would-be diplomacy, downright evasiveness, and pontification. Time-worn communication mechanisms are used solely for defensive purposes.

Individual enterprise has largely been construed to mean, and limited to, the establishment of a new business — or entrepreneurship. *This means that only a fraction of our qualified population is really living and practicing free enterprise.* Most of those men and women who have not been formally recognized by our industrial society as having top management or entrepreneurial assignments are not currently experiencing their proper measure of recognition and achievement. In fact, the basic foundations and substance of our free enterprise system are poorly understood by the great mass of employees. Yet, until the full potential of what is still a sleepy giant — our free enterprise system — is brought to full life inside our business organizations, we cannot hope for real motivation in depth.

17

LIVING FORCES AT WORK

A large insurance company was concerned about its internal climate. It seemed dead. The halls and offices were filled with well-groomed, polite, proper people. Emotion was rarely in evidence — and neither was vigor. Meetings were characterized by pleasantness, blandness, large vocabularies, and little accomplishment. At 5:00 P.M. the vast building emptied miraculously within a couple of minutes.

For some time, the chief executive had been pleased at what he assumed was evidence of a one-big-happy-family atmosphere. Here, he felt, was a fine example of group dynamics in operation, with faithful troops following his benign leadership. He began to get uneasy, however, as he saw volume inching forward while that of his competitors zoomed ahead. Also, he was shocked at the results of an internal cost analysis. But, having read a great deal about the need for sound "human relations" in business, he thought he knew what was wrong. He resolved to bring the latest techniques to bear on the company's problems.

1. He subscribed to a bulletin-board service which provided a series of cartoons and statistics designed to fire the entire workforce with new enthusiasm for the job.
2. He decreed that the house organ should be expanded and that it should include the names of more employees.
3. He initiated a number of sales contests.

4. He overhauled the contents of the reading racks.
5. He personally supervised the establishment of an evaluation plan which graded jobs primarily on the basis of a point system.
6. He increased the financial rewards provided by the suggestion system.
7. He requested that key personnel overlook no opportunity to make hearty, congratulatory comments to each other.
8. He planned a series of companywide talks in which he reaffirmed the ancient and honorable traditions of the company and reviewed its achievements.

Time passed. There were some distinct improvements, but an analysis of turnover and sales performance records clearly showed that the real producers and prime movers were steadily leaving the company — often to join much smaller and lesser-known companies. Besides, several unwritten rules still seemed to be operating:

1. Don't ruffle anybody's feelings.
2. Never rock the boat.
3. When in doubt, establish a new committee or "assistant to."
4. Show how good you are by developing new forms and writing lengthy memoranda on every possible occasion.

Something had to be done — and pretty quickly. Luckily the president realized, while there was still time, that his people wanted stretching, that a climate was needed which would motivate them to increased productivity. This meant that new concepts must be shaped; new principles evolved and applied; new habits, attitudes, and values developed to the end that all the company's resources might be fused and focused on reasonable yet demanding objectives. Then the bland could stop leading the bland.

TARGET: RESULTS

The president's new approach is sketchily outlined here:

1. He developed and communicated throughout the company a thoroughly understandable statement of his basic beliefs concerning such matters as free enterprise, the dignity of the individual, the honorable and essential role of profit, and the need for an uncompromising stand on integrity.
2. He took the lead in laying out clear overall company objectives. These had to do with —
   • Productivity.
   • Innovation.
   • Physical and financial resources.
   • Marketing.
   • Manager performance and development.
   • Worker performance and attitude.
   • Public responsibility.
   • Profitability.
3. The company's job structure was revised so that all positions were clearly defined in writing. The president vowed that henceforth he would consider

for promotion only people whose values were appropriate to a vigorous, positive, stretching environment; who were fit and tough-minded; who would bear witness that here was a company which lived and personified the beliefs expressed by its chief executive.

4. Results requirements—both qualitative and quantitative — were developed for every position. All employees must understand the *what, where, when, who, how,* and above all the *why* of their jobs.

5. The worth of every department, person, and job in the company was evaluated in terms of *contribution to the company's goals.*

   • Departmental objectives were recast so that they contributed directly to the stated goals of the company.

   • Position descriptions were converted from statements of responsibility to incorporate the new results requirements. They became dynamic instruments of management.

   • The utilization of all the company's resources in the business had to be justified on the basis of profit-center accounting.

   • Compensation had to be related directly to contribution. Traditional job evaluation, which rewards volume of activity, was abandoned.

6. All key personnel were held accountable for the results requirements of their positions, but only after they had received all information and guidance necessary to high-level performance and they

knew — in depth — the *what, where, when, who, how,* and *why* of both the company and their jobs. Yardsticks for measuring their effectiveness were developed, and they understood that they must produce the desired results or be subject to appropriate disciplinary action.

7. All management personnel were reminded of the fact that management is the development of people, not the direction of things. The new philosophy emphasized that people are the buyers of our products and services; people built the facilities and equipment we use; people run the machines and process the administrative papers that are part of our operations. Without people, as the president pointed out, the best facilities in the world are meaningless.

8. The energy, goals, and aspirations of all the people in the company — managers and nonmanagers alike — were focused on the achievement of the objectives and goals that had been spelled out. It was understood that every employee must know why the company was in business, why his department and function existed, and why he must meet certain results requirements. Only in this way could the individual worker know true job satisfaction and the manager have the feeling of being a businessman in his own right which is such an important factor in motivation.

9. All key personnel were taught the substance and application of planning, organization, coordina-

tion, execution, and control. All five steps in management must be carried out, they were told, if order, consistency, and real accomplishment were to be achieved.

10. Planned training sessions were held to help key personnel develop a practical knowledge of the principles of motivation. They were encouraged to understand and help meet the basic needs of all employees, determining the personal objectives of their subordinates and relating these goals to both departmental and company objectives. They reviewed the laws of communication, the importance of candor, the value and use of the emotional context. Always the need to build on strengths, not dwell on weaknesses, was emphasized.

Constantly the president reiterated his two main premises: (1) The only reason for being on a payroll is to produce results. (2) The total resources of a business are men, money, materials, time, and space; and their use can be justified only on the basis of *positive* results.

RESULTS ACHIEVED

As goals were set, and as the definitive steps needed to implement each one were carried out, a new climate began to build up in the company. Results were noticeable and — to the top executive — delightful. A pronounced quickening of the administrative machinery set in; politics, cliques, and superficial status indicators showed signs of melting away in the new warmth. Conversations came alive with sudden meaning; words like "purpose," "plan," "strategy," "innovation," and "timing" were heard. Cost control became an individual challenge rather than a source of cynical comment.

Many executives discovered for the first time that one of life's greatest pleasures is to be found in developing others. Emotions were assets rather than liabilities. People were *for* something because they at last saw clearly what the company was for and understood the benefit, to them, of dynamic concerted effort. Profit became an everyday word and concept all the way down through the management structure. It was freed of its associated stereotypes and became recognized for what it is — a vital ingredient of our whole way of life.

The president of the company was forewarned: he must not become unduly complacent. The new dynamism could lose momentum *if he ceased to set a good example.*

THOSE INDEFINABLE FACTORS

In contrast, the chief executive of a retail store had achieved — or thought he had achieved — the elements of a climate that should have encouraged personnel to reach for new levels of productivity. Management by objectives was already in operation, according to the chief. Each department head had carefully developed performance objectives which clearly stipulated quality, quantity, and time and were calculated to help achieve overall company objectives. A beautifully conceived set of organizational charts existed, management's expectations as spelled out in the objectives were reasonable, and the executives were highly paid. Sales volume was climbing each year, and the store was doing better than most of its competitors.

The chief executive, however, was not satisfied with his organization's progress. Morale was not high, and there was no discernible tempo or beat in the store's operations.

What was the matter?

In the first place, the rudiments of the productivity climate structure had been established, but the vital essence, the intangibles which make the difference between good and excellent management, were not there. Wisdom was still considered secondary to intelligence. Mental alertness was apparently valued more than judgment. Results were given lip service, but activity was being rewarded. The *spirit* of the organization was not being skillfully fed and nourished.

Warm, wise candor — frankness — was confused with abrasive bluntness. Managers were complaining about the weaknesses of subordinates and situations rather than deciding what could be done to capitalize on their strengths.

Second, the "I" and the "we" were still confused. The difference between being an individual and being a member of a team had not been clarified, nor had the difference between being an individual and being a rebel. Whereas the rebel is *against* things — either known or unknown — the individual is *for* things. And he knows *why*. Strong and rugged individualism is at home on the management team where the productivity climate prevails because one of the best ways to be sure what *you* are for is to think through what the *company* stands for in terms of ethical and positive goals. Mere rebelliousness — stubbornly being against something out of a sense of unhappiness or frustration — quickly arrives at the point of diminishing returns or dividends in health, happiness, and productivity. Oftener than not it is the result of poor direction. And — significantly — the rebel can by skillful direction be transformed into a sturdy, goal-oriented individual who is a real asset to the team.

Finally, in this retail store, the reasons for the existing objectives were not completely understood by all key personnel. The *why*, the values of top management, had been communicated only in part. Intangible and elusive though they were, concepts and attitudes had to be defined and built into the central administrative flow of the business before morale rose, productivity increased, and the overall improvement was noticeable.

MANAGEMENT IS A SIMPLE THING

Management with the emphasis on motivation is *effective* management. It need not and should not be complex.

One of the fallacies of our modern age is that a process or a thing must be either expensive or complex

— and preferably both — to be worthwhile. Yet from the beginning of recorded history the great breakthroughs in human understanding have been brought about by two major forces: (1) the search for truth and its application and (2) an intense desire to reduce complexity to simplicity. Management will never achieve truly significant results through motivation by placing its reliance in a set of tools and techniques alone. A realistic and very practical blending of fundamental truths applied in an orderly and planned way to the chaotic variables of modern business is the only possible approach to the emerging worldwide needs of tomorrow.

Too often, says Saul Gellerman in *Motivation and Productivity*, an individual's environment blocks his inclinations and drives him, despairing and bitter, into "a stubborn, foot-dragging negativism." Therefore, it is clear that

> Management's great task, if it is to stop the trend toward the dehumanization of work and tap man's potential more fully, is to fashion this environment into a stimulus, not a suppressor. . . .
>
> There is nothing in the free enterprise system or in the nature of man that requires work to be frustrating or to bring out the worst instead of the best in a man. [Quite the contrary!] . . .
>
> There is nothing inevitable about the nature of tomorrow's industrial world, either. It is a matter of choice. We are designing it today, whether we realize it or not, in every decision made or not made and in every precedent set, broken, or followed. . . . The basis for informed decisions

about industry's tomorrow is greater now than it has ever been before, which gives us good reason to be hopeful about the future.

THE NEED FOR SECURITY

Standing in the way of the full utilization of individual potential is, of course, the human need for security — or, to state it in reverse, the fear of insecurity which, understandably enough, has increased to such overwhelming proportions in recent decades. Middle management in particular is loaded with "security"-conscious people. Take a sampling from the commuter trains, the supper clubs, the washrooms, the shop, and the office. Ask, "Why are you working?" The usual answer — expressed or implied — is, "For security."

Let's back off and take a quick look through a big lens at the human race over the years. Originally, primitive man was insecure unless assured that he could protect himself from wild beasts and have enough food in his belly to assuage hunger pangs. Later, as evolution continued, he began to sense other needs vaguely and to be more conscious of the physical environment in which he roamed. He saw gods and goddesses in the forces of nature to which he was subject, made and worshiped idols which seemed to give him some sort of reassurance. Still later he turned from hunting and fishing to raising crops and herding cattle and sheep. He joined with other men for companionship and safety — first in nomadic groups and then in more easily defended villages and cities — for, as men became "civilized," they became acquisitive; group began to raid group and to make war on one another. In time rude walls came to be built around the villages and outlying settlements, and eventually these developed into heavily fortified towns and the turreted, moated castles of wealthy lords and barons. But, having provided for ritualistic appeasement of their gods and having protected their possessions as best they knew how, our ancestors felt that they had reached just about the limits of their responsibility so far as their own and their families' security was concerned.

Now, though, let's jump across the centuries and look at these United States through the big lens. We are surrounded with material abundance. The average man has more than adequate food and shelter. He has more than adequate transportation, leisure, and entertainment. He has fine churches, schools, and stores. And yet insecurity lurks everywhere! A deep spiritual hunger is all too prevalent. Fears sprout in our conversations and actions, in every conceivable kind of work and social situation.

What are we afraid of? Here are a few of our fears:

· We are afraid of not being liked, understood, or wanted.
· We are afraid of being ridiculed for being different.
· We are afraid of heart attacks, ulcers, nervous breakdowns.
· We are afraid to change jobs and sometimes afraid even to hold jobs.
· We are afraid to say no.

29

- We are afraid to disagree.
- We are afraid to be *for* a lot of things. It seems so much easier to be *against* things, especially when it is unpopular to take the opposing view.

Obviously, if we are to build greater security in the individual, in the business context as in any other, we must dissolve such fears. How? By personal example! A picture, they say, is worth a thousand words. *But personal example is worth a thousand pictures!*

SOURCES OF STRENGTH

Our free enterprise way of life provides more than adequate opportunity for individual dignity and individual abundance. The religious and political heritage on which it is based insures this. The Declaration of Independence and the U.S. Constitution, however, cannot do the whole job — they are just sources of strength and inspiration. Principles, laws, policies and procedures are the pipelines from these reservoirs to a group of secure people working together in an enlightened business environment. But the flow through the pipelines has been getting thinner, and the less the average employee knows about this spiritual and legal heritage and can apply it to the very practical day-to-day business of living and working, the more he will continue to build fears and fight ghosts.

Here, then, is a very real need and opportunity for the chief executive to clarify his thinking and communicate his values. This first step in establishing the productivity climate cannot be skimped.

To be sure, the normal employee benefits contributing to job security must be both adequate and effectively communicated. Salaries, bonuses, profit-sharing plans, stock options — all are important; too few companies have tapped the potential that can be gained by carefully organizing their compensation programs and the accompanying fringe benefits. It is even more important, however, that no possibility be overlooked to relate compensation, fringe benefits, and — above all — promotional opportunities directly to the achievement of results. If this vital link is overlooked, your program becomes a distinct liability rather than an asset. It encourages laziness rather than dynamism.

Still, no matter how well you do in this compensation and benefit area, your greatest potential asset — and one you probably aren't using fully — is your personal beliefs and guidelines for living defined and communicated to the far corners of the business. Only in this way can the fears that block true security be conquered.

In sum, each of us is only as secure as our image of ourself makes us. And, always, what we *are* speaks so loud that others cannot hear what we are *saying*.

IDENTIFICATION WITH THE COMPANY

Top executives report that one of their greatest frustrations is their subordinates' tendency to be primarily interested just in discharging the responsibilities of a blocked-out function on the organization chart. They do not seem to think like businessmen. They seem to see some separation between the management of their particular company area and the business which is the company's reason for being — and there is none. Management without some business to manage would be no management at all. Conversely, trying to be a businessman without managing would be equally futile. Each member of the management team must be made to realize that his success in contributing directly to the success of the business as a whole is the one big criterion for giving him additional income and perquisites.

There are several steps needed to bring this about in the productivity climate:

1. Explore the personal goals of each of your subordinate managers and determine how these can best be furthered within the company.

2. Analyze existing compensation practices; study the peculiarities of such supplementary devices as bonuses, profit sharing, pensions, and stock options; weigh carefully the contribution — in terms of motivation and increased productivity — which can be expected from each one.

3. Prepare hybrid plans, tailored to the company, as required to achieve an organized program which will stimulate sensitive reaction — under capable administration — to the requirements of both company and personal goals; that is, the accomplishment of desired results.

Of course, the various forms of supplementary compensation for executives have been assailed by a number of people, sometimes with justification. Stock-option plans, for example, are only as honest as the people who develop and administer them. Where management by integrity does not exist, dishonesty is going to crop out — if not in stock options, somewhere else.

Remember, too, that the best-conceived stock-option or pension program cannot make its greatest contribution to results without the other ingredients required in a skillfully structured climate of motivation and productivity.

Opportunity and the Search for Inner Space

At a time when our technological achievements are carrying us farther and farther into outer space, we have been lagging in our development of inner space and capacity; that is, the inner man — in a word, the space between the ears. The belief has become widely accepted that opportunity is restricted to promotions and pay raises. So much so that many members of management seem incapable of imagining what *total* development can mean.

The truth of the matter is that modern business provides us with an endless series of opportunities to contribute, to build, to develop, and to *give*. But these opportunities will continue to present themselves only to the blind side of the executive who sees opportunity as a series of *getting* rather than *giving* situations. Preoccupation with financial security to the exclusion of emotional security, the desire to advance oneself at the expense of others — these will only paralyze real opportunity for total development and success.

The executive who genuinely wants to continue to grow and become successful as a whole man will find only one true route to this goal — the development of other people and other things. Some of the building blocks required are these:

- Know yourself — but not to the point where you become absorbed with self.
- Cultivate personal dignity and respect the dignity of others.
- Develop a set of fundamental truths by which you shape your life.
- Recognize that the pursuit of ease is a hollow and empty thing totally lacking in ultimate satisfaction.
- Recognize that you can best help others define and clarify their purpose by first clarifying your own.
- Focus always on positives. Negative thinking, negative habits, and negative living have never met the test.
- Recognize that all men make mistakes but that the successful man is concerned with, not what went wrong or who was to blame, but what can be *done* about it.
- Accept your role in the American free enterprise system with eagerness and pride.
- Unfetter your imagination and scrupulously avoid

remaining local and provincial in your thinking. The world is shrinking rapidly, as we all know, and the man whose outlook is limited will find it increasingly difficult to seize and make use of opportunities.

The chance to grow and serve is not as big as you are — it's bigger. The challenge for you is to keep pace.

RECOGNITION — OF YOU AND OF HIM

There are men who achieve virtually complete financial security; they have all the money they could wish for. Many feel that they have earned a distinct place for themselves in family, company, and community and that in so doing they have already seized and utilized many opportunities. But often something is missing — something which we all must have for a truly complete life. This is recognition.

The desire for genuine recognition has frequently been confused with lack of modesty. But the two traits are quite different. Excessive modesty is simply a downgraded view of yourself, whereas self-confidence is actually self-knowledge. Until you know what you have within yourself as an individual, you cannot know what you can give. All reasonably normal people are aware of themselves. They recognize approximately what their talents and worth are, with the result that their productivity may go steadily downhill if others consistently fail to see and acknowledge their abilities. Deep, sustaining self-confidence is, in fact, one of the scarcest commodities in the world today.

In the helter-skelter rush after World War II — and, indeed, right up to the present — to train management people, primarily supervisors, in "human relations," considerable emphasis has been placed on the need for according all employees adequate recognition. Whole new businesses have sprung up to meet this need. They are engaged primarily in the merchandising of motivational devices: titles, name plates, badges, service pins, unique office furnishings, executive washrooms and dining rooms, club memberships, expense accounts, and similar aids to identification.

It has become popular to say, "We make them feel like individuals, not mere numbers," and the usual manner in which this is done is to add to the existing array of such gadgets. Yet these will consistently meet the need for recognition in only its most superficial forms. Only when each boss takes the time to sit down and develop a real understanding of his subordinates' drives and ambitions will the wellsprings of true motivation be tapped.

In its preoccupation with human relations, management has in essence attempted to administer to the symptoms rather than the causes of low productivity and lack of morale. (That's where the insurance company president went wrong.) It has tried open houses, annual reports, bulletin boards, contests, house organs, classroom instruction, newsletters, pay-envelope inserts, employee handbooks, posters, shop committees, policy and procedure manuals, reading racks, suggestion systems, and meetings of all kinds. Some of these gimmicks are next to worthless; many are more than worthwhile. Properly used, with a sincere concern for the individual and his needs, they can be highly effective motivational aids. But they are secondary, always, to the total climate within the organization.

A Two-Way Relationship

The relationship between boss and subordinate can sometimes work against recognition. For example, the controller of a food-processing firm consistently felt rebuffed and rejected by the president. The controller had the habit of assembling elaborate masses of data and presenting them to the president, always with a full explanation of how much time, effort, and strain had gone into their preparation. Viewed from his standpoint, this devotion to duty was noble and laudable, and he thought the president should realize it.

The president, however, was a busy man who wanted no more than stripped-down decision-making data — at the right time and in the right place. He found it annoying to listen to the fatuous, self-centered dissertations of the controller who, seemingly, was trying to impress him for purely personal reasons. This, he told himself, was not what the controller was being paid for.

The president eventually laid out clear results requirements for the controllership function and was able to counsel the controller candidly on the basic purpose of his job: how to make the best use of the firm's financial resources. The controller, for his part, learned how to change the whole emphasis of his department from activity to results; relate all activity to objectives, not personal and subjective feelings; and make three words work for him: thoroughness, specificity, and, above all, judgment.

Thus a new kind of warm, dynamic, and meaningful relationship began to develop between the president and the controller. And, as it grew, the controller came to feel that the president was giving him the real recognition he craved — the kind that is not contrived but is based on actual accomplishment.

PERSONAL GOALS: WHY?

Every person from the chairman of the board to the newest and greenest worker has personal goals. If this is true, why do we continue, in most companies, to ignore them?

Two reasons stand out: first, sheer laziness and lethargy; second, the fundamental fallacy that the average employee's personal goals are somehow not in tune with those of the company or, at best, are irrelevant. Because of this indifference and careless thinking, business is failing to capitalize on its greatest asset: its experienced, seasoned people.

More and more, however, we are learning to develop

and to value the goal-oriented person, the employee who knows where he is going and sees his position in the company as a means of getting there — who, indeed, could scarcely remain a part of the organization and fail to share in its objectives. In *Goal Setting: Key to Individual and Organizational Effectiveness*, Charles L. Hughes makes this point:

> Neither company nor individual can long tolerate a condition in which personal goals do not relate in some way to those established for the organization. Whatever the individual does must fit in; he must be able to perceive himself as a person seeking career objectives, and he must find these objectives within the company, or else he may choose or be forced to leave and seek them in another environment. . . .
>
> The ambitious man, moreover, will establish these personal goals with the idea of achieving them with a degree of excellence, not just perfunctorily. Like the company, he will address himself seriously to the question, "What do I want to become?"

Just what *does* this man want from his job? A quick though by no means foolproof way to find out is to ask yourself what *you* want. Early retirement and a chance to travel? Well-educated, well-adjusted responsible children? Two cars and a fine house? Money in the bank? Social prestige? The satisfaction of having served one's fellow men? What does success mean to *you*? The degree to which you achieve it will depend, in part, on what you are prepared to put into your career: brains, physical energy, moral stamina, willpower, courage, industry — all the rest.

Questions like these are thought starters that should give you some clues to your subordinates' hopes and ambitions. Of course, they're not all going to open their hearts to you automatically, and there definitely are areas into which you have no right to probe — goals that are not only personal but private. But curiosity is one thing and a sincere interest on the part of the boss is something else altogether. You are quite properly anxious that each of the people for whom you are responsible learn and grow on the job to the end that he will realize his fullest potential in the company, and in most cases he will be gratified at the chance to discuss his prospects and take a new sight on the future. Which, after all, is the purpose of the whole elaborate setup of management by objectives with its goal-setting sessions, its statements of required results, and its periodic performance appraisals.

RESULTS ARE THE KEY

Why do we work? Why do we want to continue living? The answer, surprising though it may be to many, must always be to get things done. Even the person whose principal distinguishing characteristic seems to be laziness still spends his day doing something — traditionally rocking or whittling. The main difference between the successful and the unsuccessful person is not that the one is *doing* more than the other. It consists more precisely of what he is getting *done* and, perhaps more importantly, of the fact that these achievements are positive rather than negative. Many people get a lot done, but their accomplishments are often meaningless because they are in no way related to major, positive results.

Even today we are sometimes told, "You can't measure executive performance. There are just too many intangibles." This simply isn't so — hundreds of specific performance indices have been developed. Here are a few:

- Customer complaints.
- Cost of sales.
- Cost of distribution.
- Size of orders.
- Percent of error in filling orders.
- Inventory level.
- Unit cost of materials handling.
- Dividend rates.
- Percent return on investment.
- Share of market.
- Damage claims.
- Missed delivery dates.
- Overshipments.
- Current assets to current liability.
- Percentage of surplus funds invested.
- Percent utilization of floor space.
- Ratio of inventory to assets.
- Net profit as a percentage of sales.
- Comparative accounts receivable.

- Employee turnover.
- Ratio of direct to indirect labor.
- Number of grievances.
- Number of disciplinary cases.
- Cost or time per typed letter.
- Equipment down time.
- Scrap or rejects.
- Back orders.
- Percentage of deadlines met.
- Performance against budgets or forecasts.
- Deviation from standard costs.

Some of these yardsticks are appropriate to the rank-and-file worker, some to the first-line foreman or supervisor, some to the top-level executive. A number are useful in gauging the position of the company as a whole at a given time. For the most part, however, these result indicators are quantitative. Here, by way of contrast, are some qualitative ones:

- Leadership in developing an atmosphere marked by good communication and positive mental attitudes.
- Superior performance on the part of subordinates.
- Significant ideas or breakthroughs contributed, especially when generated from outside sources.
- Self-generated personal development programs.

Dormant resources lie unused in all of us. The best way to make sure they are utilized most effectively is to know just what they should accomplish. A homely case in point is that of the typical husband-wife team setting out to rearrange the living room. Repeatedly the wife changes her mind; increasingly the husband begins to feel inept, frustrated, or just plain irritated. The end result is two frayed tempers and some quite unnecessary fatigue. What a difference when the wife has taken the time to work out in detail the finished result she visualizes and then takes the trouble to describe the new arrangement to her husband. With some ingenuity and resourcefulness he can usually get the job done quickly — minus irritations.

Develop Big Men

The man who is truly big in terms of accomplishment and leadership potential has many doors and opportunities open to him. What can you do to be sure that your management team is composed, not of little men (they may be strapping physical specimens) who are full of fears and absorbed in their own interests, but of men who are big, who are true individualists yet function like real team members?

It takes more than wishing. If you talk to your chief production executive only about production objectives and methods and do not relate these to company objectives, you encourage him to be something less than a full member of the team. He may even come to believe that production is the only company function that matters. If he is to feel a vested interest in the total fortunes of the business, it is important that he become as broad-gauge a person as is logically possible.

The personnel director who knows a good bit about production, finance, marketing, and general management is a better personnel director than the narrow specialist. He is motivated by the total climate rather than his own little empire. In the same way, the marketing director who can appreciate the difficulties of manufacturing a product which meets exacting time, quality, and quantity requirements is a better marketing director than the one who is interested only in marketing objectives and problems.

The best top financial officer is the one who has done his homework and been around enough to know that conservative, financially impeccable procedures may be comfortable but ineffectual because of a mass of sales, production, and personnel variables. He is the kind of "pro" needed by the successful business. Such a man often is able to counsel the president when to take vigorous and even risky steps in the interest of both sound management and increased profit. There are still too many financial executives who see themselves as self-righteous money *hoarders* rather than as energetic money *makers*.

An executive, moreover, spends only a portion of his total life on the job. But actually the two parts of his existence are pretty much indivisible. Each role becomes a partial product of the other. The person who concentrates steadfastly on becoming a bigger and better total person in body, mind, and spirit will make a much greater contribution to his employer than the man who "turns off" completely each evening and weekend. And he reaps appropriately big rewards. The whole man goes to work; the whole man comes home. There is no dichotomy.

BUSINESS OR INSTITUTION?

There's an old saying that declares, "We're a non-profit organization — although that isn't the way we intended it." This hoary chestnut is usually offered humorously, but many so-called businesses are in this precise category.

An old and widely respected manufacturer of leather products was having trouble making money. The company was known from coast to coast. The quality of its products was unquestioned, but it was in trouble.

The marketing director always looked for a pleasant, comforting way, however oblique it might be, to communicate with the production manager. He was heard to explain on several occasions, "He's a nice old guy. Why upset him?"

The purchasing director was an amiable, bland executive who loved to be wined and dined by salesmen. He judged most people by their school ties and social connections.

The president felt that management consisted largely of analyzing data to determine what had gone *wrong*. He devoted little time and effort to determining how to make things *better*. He felt, further, that the way to insure high employee morale was to grant additional fringe benefits or increase old ones. Most of his employees had come to consider that *benefits* were *rights* to which they were entitled.

Salary rates were based almost completely on what kind of pay would be required to hire any sort of successor. People were regarded as necessary but not important; the belief prevailed that most people are looking for an easy and restful path through life. As a result, shop and office employees were apathetic and listless. They seldom knew where they stood or who was boss. When discipline was necessary, they seldom knew why.

In attempting to hang onto every old customer, the company was carrying out many intricate manual operations which consistently lost money. Management was trying to please everyone; and, in trying to please everybody, it succeeded in pleasing practically nobody. There was a sense of urgency and anxiety at all times, but people seemed to be working at loose or unrelated ends. They were using job-shop methods to compete with production-line methods, manufacturing three times as many separate items as subsequent study revealed they should.

The company's top management group had long clung stubbornly to the stand that its high-quality hand-crafted products were greatly superior to the machine-produced items of its competitors — and they were. But 80 percent of the firm's customers couldn't tell the difference. They looked only at price, and the competition could obviously mass-produce what was wanted at a much lower price.

Although top management seemed interested in profit, the word was seldom heard or understood at lower levels.

In short, the whole business was steadily wasting away in spite of high-quality work, a good reputation, and the expenditure of much energy. Management labored under the same fallacy that has blighted the productivity of many businesses and has made useless the activities of many seminars on motivation: the fallacy that man's basic drive is to get rather than to give. This was a high price to pay for blindly continuing to take pride in the company and its products as an institution, a tradition, instead of being concerned with its future as a business.

LEADERSHIP PLUS

In summary, if free enterprise is to make the maximum contribution to the success of a business, each member of the management team must satisfy his needs for —

1. Security.
2. Belonging and identification.
3. Opportunity.
4. Recognition.

He must have that faith in himself which is the very essence of leadership and without which he cannot instill self-confidence in others and inspire them to the sort of team effort that's the sum total of its members' individual efforts — and something more. He must know the results expected of him and his department and have a good idea how best to accomplish them. He must understand the company's goals, he must have harmonized his own goals with them, and he must be able to help his subordinates examine their hopes and expectations realistically and seek personal fulfillment in the achievement of organizational objectives.

Without such leadership, a business is simply a drifting, aimless, dispirited arrangement of men, money, materials, time, and space. The problem is to make it a living, breathing entity.

SECTION TWO

Design

The Sequence (Phase 1: Study of Present Climate. Phase 2: Development of Management Philosophy. Phase 3: Development and Establishment of Objectives. Phase 4: Organization Planning, Development, and Design. Phase 5: Performance Planning and Results Requirements. Phase 6: Communication and Motivation. Phase 7: Control). The Loop Closed

Another management theory? Another program? Another sure-fire gimmick? The bemused executive surely is entitled to retort, "Who needs it? What I want is a real 'feel' for proven ways to make the whole business throb and hum. *Profit* — that's the name of the game! I've read about 'tools' and 'techniques' till I'm blue in the face."

The businessman doesn't want and doesn't need gimmicks. He is charged with accountability for developing a *total* company which accomplishes significant things to achieve *total* objectives. He must know how to energize that company from top to bottom and side to side. He must be able to stimulate involvement and commitment on the part of his employees. First — to review a little — he must communicate his philosophy and beliefs, his goals and objectives, throughout the organization. Then he must institute appropriate procedures to make sure his people meet and exceed their commitments. And he must insure that both philosophy and procedures are continuously updated in response to a rapidly changing world.

What brand of scheme, design, mechanism, or system can be developed which will give the paper-plagued executive perspective, clarity, and simplicity? Let's call it a *servo-climate* for results.

THE SEQUENCE

The seven-phase program compactly presented in Figure 1 illustrates the sequence, the flow, and, most importantly, the dynamic on-going process of management.

What is this process, really? It has been defined in numerous ways, some of which have seemed particularly apt and achieved widespread popularity. For instance: "Management is the efficient and economical use of men, money, materials, time, and space to achieve predetermined objectives." And: "Management is the development of people, not the direction of things." But, for our purposes here, let's assume another sort of definition:

> *Management is an ever-changing, ever-dynamic system of interacting minds.*

To go on with this train of thought: Our services or products are only as good as the people who make or provide them. Our people are only as good as the quality of their minds. Their minds are only as viable as the basic beliefs and values which they conceive. The top executive is only as effective as his ability to stimulate, develop, fuse, and focus these minds on meaningful results-compelling performance standards which are components of company objectives of understandable excellence.

Thus the top executive — whether head of a company, a major division, or a department — must be the fountainhead, the source of the organization's spirit and the guiding intelligence behind its direction. He must be able to *think*, to formulate a set of living and operational values into an operational system which provides parameters, stretch, and meaning for all. This is the kind of system that is exemplified by Figure 1.

Phase 1: Study of present climate. First of all we must take a long clear-eyed look at our present organizational environment. Are vested, entrenched, and nonproductive interests involved? Does everybody in the organization — all the way down — understand the anatomy, the undergirding of profit? Does everybody understand the basic beliefs and values of the top executive, the man who sets the style and tone for the organization? Do people know what company, divisions, departments, and individuals are *for?* Or are they primarily influenced by what each of these organizational elements is *against?* Are people doing things *to* each other or *for* each other? Is the profit contribution of all major resources being measured? Why? (Or why not?)

Has the policy manual been ruthlessly subjected to the big lens recently? Are policies simple, crisp, meaningful, up to date, and squarely welded into the philosophy, goals, and objectives of the enterprise?

Is the organizational structure truly functional? It

FIGURE 1

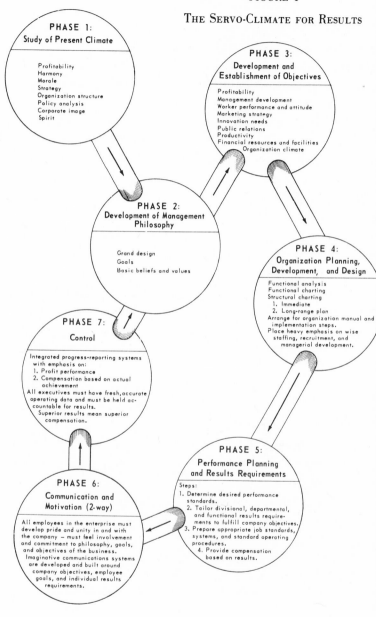

The Servo-Climate for Results

PHASE 1:
Study of Present Climate

Profitability
Harmony
Morale
Strategy
Organization structure
Policy analysis
Corporate image
Spirit

PHASE 3:
Development and
Establishment of Objectives

Profitability
Management development
Worker performance and attitude
Marketing strategy
Innovation needs
Public relations
Productivity
Financial resources and facilities
Organization climate

PHASE 2:
Development of Management
Philosophy

Grand design
Goals
Basic beliefs and values

PHASE 4:
Organization Planning,
Development, and Design

Functional analysis
Functional charting
Structural charting
1. Immediate
2. Long-range plan
Arrange for organization manual and
implementation steps.
Place heavy emphasis on wise
staffing, recruitment, and
managerial development.

PHASE 7:
Control

Integrated progress-reporting systems
with emphasis on:
1. Profit performance
2. Compensation based on actual
achievement
All executives must have fresh, accurate
operating data and must be held accountable for results.
Superior results mean superior
compensation.

PHASE 5:
Performance Planning
and Results Requirements

Steps:
1. Determine desired performance
standards.
2. Tailor divisional, departmental,
and functional results requirements to fulfill company objectives.
3. Prepare appropriate job standards,
systems, and standard operating
procedures.
4. Provide compensation
based on results.

PHASE 6:
Communication and
Motivation (2-way)

All employees in the enterprise must
develop pride and unity in and with
the company — must feel involvement
and commitment to philosophy, goals,
and objectives of the business.
Imaginative communications systems
are developed and built around
company objectives, employee
goals, and individual results
requirements.

may not be ideal — nor need it be — in the "classic principles of organization" sense, but is it really operational and effective? Is it delivering the goods? Are there organizational appendages and offshoots that aren't contributing?

What are the "feel" and the "sense" of the climate? Are there system, order, pride in product, work area, and personal appearance? Or do we see cluttered ashtrays, sloppy desks, haggard, red-eyed managers — all the signs of overpermissiveness and lack of standards? What are the *real* problems? What do people *really* think? A carefully constructed attitude questionnaire can provide meaningful clues to the prevailing level of harmony, understanding, and performance, as well as useful information for continually updating and achieving greater excellence in philosophy, objectives, organization structure, communication, and controls.

It takes real courage to take a methodical in-depth look at the present posture of your business, but no truly dedicated, tough-minded executive will dispense with this vital step. (A checklist like the one shown as Exhibit A should prove useful.) He may feel he must brace himself for the shock of the findings — and perhaps some of them may be unpleasant — but to ignore even a vague fear that all is not well, to proceed to deploy large amounts of resources without such an analysis has consigned many companies to the corporate boneyard.

The essence of the servo-climate is lost unless management has the courage to require a constant flow of relevant facts and then act on them.

Phase 2: Development of management philosophy.

Every top executive has a grand design, whether he understands it and can articulate it or not. The point is that it should be clearly thought out, put in writing, and communicated so pervasively and so meaningfully that it provides invaluable fuel for dedication and commitment on the part of each and every employee. It is the foundation, the footings, which after all determine pretty closely just how tall a building can be. Similarly, it is the grand design — the basic philosophy — which determines the organization's scope and purpose, the heights of service and profitability to which it may eventually rise. Thus:

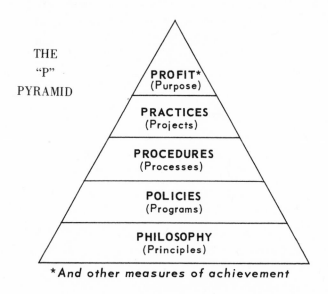

THE "P" PYRAMID

PROFIT* (Purpose)

PRACTICES (Projects)

PROCEDURES (Processes)

POLICIES (Programs)

PHILOSOPHY (Principles)

*And other measures of achievement

The failure of managers and employees alike to understand this grand design — and, in particular, the reluctance of whole segments of our society to relish the word "profit" — stem directly from their misunderstanding of the relationships involved and the full meaning of profit. It of course implies not only economic profit but social, political, and spiritual profit. The organization that plans for and proceeds on the basis of the individual dignity of human beings — whose climate contributes to a total "profit framework" — not only has nothing to apologize for when profits grow large but has, instead, a virtual obligation to radiate an intense pride in so thoroughly American an achievement.

Understandably, this concept of company philosophy and its role is not altogether compatible with the personalities of some managers and the crucial determinants of some companies' development. The distillation of beliefs and principles is, admittedly, an after-the-fact process. Successful managements know from experience, however, that it can provide much food for meaningful thought and lead to renewed and intensified commitment.

The resulting draft should be thoroughly analyzed, evaluated, criticized, and synthesized. Then the most appropriate version, variation, or hybrid should be adopted (see Exhibit B). It should also be used — disseminated to every department and every man in the company. And it must, of course, be revised and updated as indicated by the feedback of control data.

These values and beliefs which comprise the philosophical foundation for the grand design provide the mainstream, the arterial system, of the business. This draws constantly on the vast mental reservoir which holds the combined power of managerial minds in action. Each executive thus finds himself better equipped for policy interpretation and usage which *get the job done*. To harness and channel this power — to be sure that eight minds add up to more than the sum of their individual potential — is the never-ending challenge of the first-rate chief executive.

Phase 3: Development and establishment of objectives. Much has been written about the setting of objectives — but too little about the process of participation by which they are arrived at. There is a tendency to confuse permissiveness, abdication, and co-determination with appropriate involvement.

The workforce — whether managerial, technical, or hourly paid — represents a vast amount of experience, ideas, and down-to-earth judgment. The top executive needs to use this, but with the understanding that he and he alone is accountable in the final tally for the results achieved. Thus he listens, discusses, studies, and then approves corporate objectives which embody the best thinking of his staff, but which he has pared, condensed, or expanded as may be advisable. These objectives of course stem directly from the corporate philosophy and are in full consonance with it; if this is not the case, something is clearly out of phase and needs attention.

The top executive also requires the members of his immediate staff to utilize a similar process of involvement with their own subordinates, again with the understanding that they alone will be accountable for the achievement of the results to which they commit their respective departments. Exhibit C illustrates one sound, though abbreviated, type of outline which can convert pie-in-the-sky dreams to definitive timetables for accomplishment. And it provides something else that is too seldom mentioned in management literature: peace of mind.

Phase 4: Organization planning, development, and design. All executives responsible to any significant degree for formulating or manning an organization structure should be guided by the premise that the only purpose of organization is to achieve objectives. Every company, every department and division, has organization whether management knows it or not. It's by no means essential to have an elaborate chart to hang on the wall. The important thing is to make sure that the arrangement be both logical and practical, that it focus people's efforts solely on the achievement of meaningful long- and short-range goals. The need for keeping fat out of the organization requires little elaboration. The steps shown for Phase 4 are listed sequentially and should be critically and carefully carried out.

1. *Functional analysis:* Component operations or sub-responsibilities should be grouped under each major function so that the overall arrangement afford a clear view of the activity-anatomy of that portion of the company under study — or of the entire organizational superstructure, if this is appropriate. The executive in charge may be required to complete appropriate questionnaires and analysis sheets.

2. *Functional charting:* The analysis of the operations or components of each function, and their disposition, should be strongly conditioned by —
   a. Analysis yardsticks:
      (1) Eliminate?
      (2) Combine?
      (3) Rearrange?
      (4) Synthesize?
      (5) Simplify?
   b. The evaluation yardstick; that is, *contribution to company objectives.*

   The new organization which emerges should then meet all sound tough-minded management criteria.

3. *Structural charting:* The end result of careful pragmatic study, this should be manualized and disseminated in a manner most appropriate for the particular company climate or environment. The completed chart must reflect the dynamic quality of the informal organization, or the "formal" structure will not be truly effective.

Sound organization planning calls for a long-range structure designed to meet the needs of your long-range objectives just as surely as your present or newly evolving structure must meet the requirements of your short- and medium-range objectives. Staffing is always critical. Selection criteria should be based on statements of desired results which have been developed solely for the purpose of achieving company objectives. A strong value system should be required basic equipment for the budding executive. Remember: *He will be only as effective as the quality of his mind permits, and the quality of his mind will be no better than the values which comprise it.*

Development programs should emphasize learning by doing. Both young and experienced managers should accustom themselves to being judged by what they accomplish through the practical application of their basic beliefs and principles.

Phase 5: Performance planning and results requirements. Figure 2 illustrates a dynamic method for determining performance requirements. It also illustrates, in microcosm, the never-ending process of continuous updating, reassessment, refinement, and stretch implicit in the total servo-climate approach.

Setting performance standards is not, and never can be, a tool or technique in itself. Standards must be evoked by a dynamic process of involvement, or the hoped-for commitment is only a paper tiger.

The tendency to consider the establishment of performance standards or results requirements as a mere mechanistic exercise or discipline is responsible for the fact that many attempts at management by results are falling far short of their optimum potential because of failure to lay the foundation systematically for a results *climate.* The individual executive's standards are not fully meaningful to *him.* He doesn't understand their *what, where, when, who,* or how or, above all, *why* he is expected to operate according to a system of commitments.

Too often we hear businessmen comment, "We tried the 'technique' of management by objectives, but it didn't meet our expectations." Or, "Theory Y is fine in prin-

FIGURE 2: THE SERVO-MECHANISM OF INDIVIDUAL PERFORMANCE STANDARDS

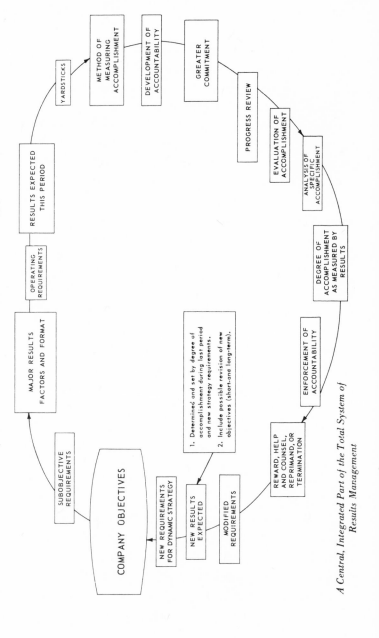

A Central, Integrated Part of the Total System of Results Management

ciple, but I don't know how we would integrate it into the mainstream of the business." Or, "The 'managerial grid' is a fascinating 'tool,' but running a business involves *all* its resources — not just people."

Accountability is the gadfly, the catalyst. Exhibit D shows one format for pulling together the activities of executives into a position description which is an integral part of a results-compelling servo-system and which, if administered with guts and integrity, is virtual proof against company politics.

Phase 6: Communication and motivation. Effective communication cannot be willed, ordered, or legislated overnight. It must be *earned*, and it can be earned only by a top management group that is not confusing intelligence with wisdom. The intelligent executive can often articulate brilliantly without ever being understood. Thus, not only is the effect largely wasted, but it increasingly builds up a backwash of frustration and cynicism.

The truly wise executive may not be superbly articulate, but his primary goal is understanding. Accordingly, not only is he concerned with what *he* wants as an individual, but he places heavy stress on the relationships among company, departmental, and individual goals. He doesn't say, "Shape up or ship out," until he has made every logical effort to insure that employees understand the new, up-to-date meaning of the old phrase, "Take care of the company and it will take care of you." The wise subordinate sees readily that it's to his advantage to recognize the interaction between company and personal goals — and luckily, since without his commitment performance standards, results requirements, and statements of responsibility and accountability cannot have real teeth.

Considerable care must be taken in the servo-climate to insure that all appropriate handbooks, manuals, bulletin boards, meeting agenda, house organs, and other communication devices are solidly constructed around the grand design, the goals and objectives, and the organizational requirements of the business. The question must be asked constantly:

- Is it window dressing? An investment in managerial ego? Or —
- Will it make a discernible contribution to objectives?

In short, all communication must point toward both the immediate and the ultimate purposes of the company at all times.

When the majority of employees realize clearly that the action needed to accomplish their performance requirements also is the action best calculated to achieve their own goals, you have the principal elements of a highly charged motivational climate.

Phase 7: Control. The conceptual underpinning for control in the servo-climate is based on these premises:

Planning	1. A business exists only for accomplishment.
	2. People work within a business only for accomplishment.
	3. Resources are employed only for accomplishment.

Planning (*concluded*)	4. The right combination and balance of resources is needed for accomplishment.
Organization, *Coordination,* and *Execution*	5. These resources must work in consonance with each other for accomplishment.

Therefore,

Control	The effectiveness of these foregoing steps is measured *only* by accomplishment.

Control is optimum only when people know their jobs, are motivated by the climate in which they work, and understand the reasons for their commitments.

Perhaps the greatest arch-enemy of a good control system — indeed, of the management of the whole enterprise — is a too-common blend of rigidity, complacency, and permissiveness. Discipline — particularly *self*-discipline — is vital. So is watchfulness on the part of the chief executive. When performance appears to be slowing down, the tough-minded manager will more than ever want to reassure himself that —

- The grand design is still valid and is still generating its full motive voltage.
- Overall objectives are still sound, and all key personnel understand them.
- The end results required of each major function are set up in the way most conducive to accomplishing those objectives.
- Communication is effective — both downward and upward.
- Other elements of the servo-climate are "synap-

sing" — coalescing in a live, stimulating atmosphere conducive to renewed inspiration and enthusiasm.

FIGURE 3

EVOLUTION OF THE SERVO-CLIMATE

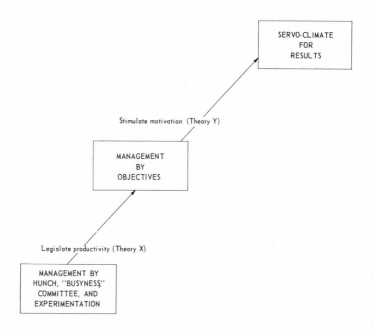

Perhaps there are as many formats for key items of control data as there are key executives managing key functions or companies. Exhibit E illustrates one grouping designed to reflect the performance of the organization. No effort has been made here to present a control sheet for any particular *kind* of company. Rather, the format is intended simply to help the executive who requires a sensitive, timely, appropriately synchronized flow of performance data from his team. Such an executive is usually well advised to structure his master control document with these criteria in mind:

· Versatility.
· Simplicity.
· Understandability.
· Accuracy.
· Relevance to strategy.

Remember, the *best* control is enlightened, involved, and committed individuals.

The Loop Closed

And so the loop closes. As it pulses back to Phase 2 (see Figure 1) again and proceeds to the necessary modification and updating of Phases 3, 4, 5, 6, and 7, the most important consideration to keep in mind is that the future of the business — not to mention our entire economic and social system — rests squarely, if sometimes uneasily, on the man who can *think;* who can then *articulate, communicate,* and *relate* the diverse elements of the enterprise into a reciprocating, perpetual *whole.* And, always, his most crucial challenge must be *development* — of himself, his colleagues, and his enterprise.

About 75 percent of U.S. companies today manage by hunch, by sheer activity or "busyness," by such devices as committees, and by frank experimentation. (See

Figure 3.) Realizing that something is lacking, they apply Theory X (to use Douglas McGregor's term); because they assume that their employees must be coaxed or coerced into working, they try to legislate productivity. Then, at a somewhat later stage of development, they read about management by objectives and install its full apparatus of goals and results requirements. About 20 percent of American firms have taken this step, which still is not enough. It is after a disciplined refinement of McGregor's Theory Y has been introduced, after deliberate steps have been taken to stimulate motivation, to make the individual see the importance of an all-out effort to both himself and the company, that the right climate, the servo-climate, begins to become a reality. True commitment is not possible unless preceded by involvement and *conviction*. Possibly 5 percent of the companies in the United States have achieved it.

The servo-climate for results must not be confused with a mere warmed-over or updated version of Theory Y. It marks a distinct pragmatic step *beyond* Theory Y. It harnesses the *closed loop!*

With the effective development and implementation of the servo-climate, the nerves and muscles form on the corporate bones and management by objectives becomes a fundamental part, but only a part, of a total system of management.

Guides

Exhibit A: General Climate Analysis. Exhibit B: Company Philosophy and Beliefs (Sample Statement). Exhibit C: Procedure for Reviewing Objectives and Strategies. Exhibit D: Simplified and Condensed Format for an Executive Position Description. Exhibit E: An Integrated Progress-Reporting System

EXHIBIT A

GENERAL CLIMATE ANALYSIS

POLICIES

	Yes	*No*	*Why?*
1. Are policies clearly defined and in manual form?	____	____	____
2. Do they accurately reflect the philosophy and "grand design" of the company?	____	____	____

PLANNING

1. Have company objectives and standards been thoroughly defined for —

	Yes	*No*	*Why?*
Productivity?	____	____	____
Innovation?	____	____	____
Physical and financial resources?	____	____	____
Marketing?	____	____	____
Manager performance and development?	____	____	____
Worker performance and attitude?	____	____	____
Public responsibility?	____	____	____
Profitability?	____	____	____

	Yes	*No*	*Why?*

2. Have PERT or Critical Path methods been used to good advantage in planning? ____ ____ ____

3. Are the following steps being taken with a view to profit maximization:

Study of all unusual expenditures and all changes and additions in product, policy, methods, systems, and equipment in light of the long-term as well as the short-term effect on the company? ____ ____ ____

Continuous, organized effort to improve quality and reduce costs as well? ____ ____ ____

(Such effort must be redoubled at those times when the company is most prosperous and its operations are most profitable.)

Continuous development of all products and services, and of inspection standards, to accelerate improvements? ____ ____ ____

Continuous simplification and improvement of existing philosophies, policies, methods, and systems? ____ ____ ____

	Yes	No	Why?

Installation of fundamentally new systems, methods, and mechanizations wherever needed?

Continuous fundamental research on all phases of the company's products and related problems?

Development of new products and methods of merchandising and distribution encouraged as indicated by market requirements and overall profit value to the company?

Market investigation of the acceptability or nonacceptability of the company's products and methods of merchandising and distribution?

Routine, scheduled visits to other plants in both related and unrelated industries to examine and evaluate their policies, equipment, methods, and systems with a view to adaptation and application to the company?

Encouragement for executives and other employees to take an active part in trade and civic organizations?

	Yes	*No*	*Why?*

Provision of adequate capital for current and future plans? ___ ___ ___

4. Are business games and simulation techniques used? ___ ___ ___

How?

OPERATIONS

1. Procurement

   Are all materials purchased by competitive bid, in accordance with specifications, in quantities requisitioned by production control (if applicable)? ___ ___ ___

2. Production control and scheduling

   Is production completely planned and scheduled in accordance with marketing requirements and manufacturing facilities? ___ ___ ___

3. Plant engineering

   Is plant location determined by studies of material and labor supply and market location? ___ ___ ___

   Are plant facilities arranged in accordance with production methods and processes? ___ ___ ___

Guides

4. Tool engineering

   Are tools developed, designed, ____ ____ ____
   and tested to yield the lowest
   feasible manufacturing cost for
   each product?

5. Manufacturing

   Are high-quality, low-cost prod- ____ ____ ____
   ucts the rule?

   How is this determined?

   Are modern methods of plant ____ ____ ____
   layout used?

   What ones?

   What is proportion of direct labor to indirect labor?

   How much production is pres-
   ently scrap?

   How measured?

   Are schedules met?   ____ ____ ____

   How far are they planned in
   advance?

   Are methods improvements at- ____ ____ ____
   tempted?

	Yes	*No*	*Why?*

Check method used:

   Flow process charts   ____

   Layout and flow diagrams ____

   Work distribution analysis____

   Time and motion studies   ____

   Other   ____

6. Quality control

Is quality control a separate func- ____ ____ ____
tion?

Is quality control used as an aid ____ ____ ____
to sales and manufacturing?

How?

Are deviations from quality speci- ____ ____ ____
fications permitted during peri-
ods of peak delivery requirements?

Has quality control improved ____ ____ ____
the design of products and proc-
esses?

How?

Have possible applications of ____ ____ ____
statistical quality control been
studied?

| | Yes | No | Why? |

7. Value analysis assurance

Are any or all of the foregoing functions being analyzed 100% in terms of value contribution?

8. Product/service analysis

Have the specific product lines or services been determined which will yield the greatest return for the resources expended?

Gather and chart the following sales data:

Sales by product line (last 5 years)

Gross profit by product line (last 5 years)

Share of market by product line (last 5 years)

Total market by product line

Gather and chart the following distribution data:

Sales and gross profit by channel of distribution (last 5 years)

Sales and gross profit by customer (Pareto analysis should

show that 20% of customers
account for 80% of sales.)

Analyze the allocation of the
company's resources with respect
to its sources of greatest profit.

Identify the transactions which
generate costs and measure their
variability by product line. For
example:

Number of sales orders proc-
essed

Number of factory orders issued

Number of invoices sent out

GENERAL CONTROL

1. Is there a system of standard
costs?

2. Does it reflect all variances between standard and actual costs?

3. Are variances from standard
performance supplied currently to management?

4. Are there unnecessary accounting records?

	Yes	No	Why?
Has this been analyzed recently?	___	___	___

5. Are all control records integrated? ___ ___ ___

6. Are estimates for product pricing based on standard costs? ___ ___ ___

7. Is provision made for management to keep currently informed on the effect of sales mixture and product selling prices on total company profits? ___ ___ ___

8. Are breakeven charts used by each major department to reflect the effect of additional volume on cost and profit? ___ ___ ___

9. Are there budgetary controls? ___ ___ ___

10. Is there an adequate system of reports on the performance of all departments? ___ ___ ___

11. Is there a system of commitments? ___ ___ ___

12. Are operative research administrative procedures, records, forms, and reports designed to produce required information at lowest cost? ___ ___ ___

	Yes	*No*	*Why?*

Discuss examples.

13. Are accounting data supplied promptly, in the form best adapted to use by management? ___ ___ ___

Is modern accounting equipment used? ___ ___ ___

14. Are perpetual inventories and stock control maintained? ___ ___ ___

15. For what length of time are forecasts prepared?

16. Are controls too few? ___ ___ ___

Or are they too numerous? ___ ___ ___

17. Are controls *understood?* ___ ___ ___

18. Are controls dynamic instruments for profit maximization? ___ ___ ___

HUMAN RELATIONS

1. What are people doing TO each other?

2. What are people doing FOR each other?

3. Do members believe in the purpose of the organization? ___ ___ ___

Guides

	Yes	No	Why?
4. Do they believe in their leadership?	____	____	____
5. Do they believe in each other?	____	____	____
6. Do they communicate and participate effectively?	____	____	____
7. Do they feel free to express their views?	____	____	____
8. Do they believe in the company?	____	____	____
9. Is the executive group cohesive?	____	____	____

10. Who helps whom?

    Who goes to whom?

11. What executives appear to be only partially accepted?

    Why?

12. What kinds of personal adjustment problems are there?

13. Are bosses too busy to see their people?	____	____	____
14. Are subordinates afraid of their bosses?	____	____	____

15. What kinds of friction are there?

    Why?

ORGANIZATION STRUCTURE

	Yes	*No*	*Why?*
1. Does it work effectively?	____	____	____

By what yardsticks?

| 2. Does the informal organization work against the formal organization? | ____ | ____ | ____ |

How?

3. What kind of informal subgroups or cliques have been formed?

4. What marked splits are there between various levels of management or between management and employees?

5. What is the social hierarchy?

What are the status symbols?

| 6. Do people understand and accept the organization structure, line of command, and delegation of authority and responsibility? | ____ | ____ | ____ |

| 7. Do individuals have an opportunity to use their initiative and demonstrate their ability to grow? | ____ | ____ | ____ |

	Yes	*No*	*Why?*

8. How accurately do formal job descriptions, organization charts, or performance standards reflect the jobs of executives as *they* themselves describe them?

9. Is the organization structure simple and flexible? ____ ____ ____

   Or is it inflexible and complex? ____ ____ ____

10. Are subordinate units relatively self-sufficient? ____ ____ ____

11. Have levels of supervision been kept to a minimum? ____ ____ ____

12. Has the number of specialized activities been kept to a minimum? ____ ____ ____

13. Are all executive positions, including first-line positions, truly management positions? ____ ____ ____

14. In moving up, have executives taken important parts of their old duties with them? ____ ____ ____

15. Are waste effort and waste motion common? ____ ____ ____

    Where?

	Yes	*No*	*Why?*

16. Can key decisions be made at relatively low levels? ____ ____ ____

MANAGEMENT EFFECTIVENESS

1. Is there any evidence of in-depth planning? ____ ____ ____

   What kind?

2. Do executives direct, delegate, and coordinate effectively? ____ ____ ____

3. Do they initiate effective action and work with others coopera-tively? ____ ____ ____

4. Are they committed to the de-velopment of people? ____ ____ ____

5. Do people know where they stand with their superiors? ____ ____ ____

6. Do executives tend to procras-tinate over critical decisions? ____ ____ ____

   Why?

   What is the decision-making process?

7. Is the organization drifting? ____ ____ ____

   Are its energies fragmented? ____ ____ ____

84

	Yes	No	Why?

8. Is the leadership process auto-
cratic? ____ ____ ____

   Permissive and overly partici-
pative? ____ ____ ____

   Tough-minded? ____ ____ ____

9. Are any executives concerned ____ ____ ____
about working relationships
among their subordinates?

   Why?

10. Is there any evidence that ex- ____ ____ ____
ecutives are at all concerned
about self-development?

   What?

11. How do subordinate executives ____ ____ ____
view superior executives?

EFFICIENCY OF WORK METHODS

1. Are executives methods-consci- ____ ____ ____
ous and economy-minded?

2. Are standard operating proce- ____ ____ ____
dures disorganized?

   Is their purpose understood? ____ ____ ____

3. Are written instructions meticu- ____ ____ ____
lous and thorough?

	Yes	*No*	*Why?*
4. Do written instructions appear to conform to present methods?	___	___	___
5. Have jobs been simplified to the point where people can no longer have any real interest in their work?	___	___	___
6. What areas appear to be most suited for methods improvement?			
7. Can work layout be improved?	___	___	___
8. Do people show any evidence of being conscious of or interested in improving their work?	___	___	___
9. Is PERT, CPM, or Value Analysis being used?	___	___	___
10. Is the relationship of procedures to objectives understood?	___	___	___

QUALITY OF PERSONNEL PRACTICES

1. How are individual executives and employees selected?

   What criteria are used?

2. Has the selection procedure been formalized in writing? ___ ___ ___

3. Are tests used? ___ ___ ___

	Yes	No	Why?
Are these current and appropriate?	____	____	____

4. What provision is there for training and development?

5. What is the basis for promotion?

6. Do pay rates correspond to levels of work? ____ ____ ____

7. Have salary ranges been developed on the basis of activity or result factors? ____ ____ ____

8. Are all employees kept informed about company matters? ——— ——— ———

   Do they feel they are an integral part of the company? ____ ____ ____

9. How do people feel about their jobs?

10. Are they, generally speaking, in the right jobs? ____ ____ ____

11. Have supervisors and executives been selected for their leadership ability? ____ ____ ____

12. Are personnel policies continually reviewed for pertinence and relevancy? ____ ____ ____

	Yes	No	Why?

13. Are they incorporated in manuals and distributed? ____ ____ ____

14. Is the incompetent person kept on his job? ____ ____ ____

    Or have definite steps been taken to eliminate him? ____ ____ ____

15. Is there a program of job evaluation? ____ ____ ____

    Is it achievement- or activity-oriented? ____ ____ ____

16. How are staff people used?

17. Are staff and line functions discernibly different? ____ ____ ____

18. Do morale and discipline seem satisfactory? ____ ____ ____

    Is this reflected in the company's safety record? ____ ____ ____

UNION-MANAGEMENT RELATIONS

1. What is the attitude toward the contract?

2. What period of time is covered by the contract?

	Yes	No	Why?

3. How are relationships with the union representatives?

4. Are union rules being followed in spirit as well as word? ___ ___ ___

   Are these rules understood? ___ ___ ___

5. Is there any evidence of insincere practices designed to undermine the union's position? ___ ___ ___

6. Do employees view the union as their protector? ___ ___ ___

7. Is there cooperation with, rather than appeasement of, the union? ___ ___ ___

8. Is there co-determination? ___ ___ ___

BOARD OF DIRECTORS

1. Do present directors have a grasp of company problems? ___ ___ ___

2. Are they a sound blend of broad-gauge and specialized people? ___ ___ ___

3. What are their backgrounds?

4. Are they identified strongly with the company? ___ ___ ___

5. How are directors compensated?

6. Is emphasis on —

	Yes	No	Why?
Policy determination? %_____	___	___	___
Future planning? %_____	___	___	___
Current operational problems? %_____	___	___	___
External conditions? %_____	___	___	___
Internal conditions? %_____	___	___	___
Profit planning? %_____	___	___	___

7. Is there an —

	Yes	No	Why?
Audit committee?	___	___	___
Compensation committee?	___	___	___
Nominating committee?	___	___	___
Executive committee?	___	___	___

GENERAL ADMINISTRATION

1. Are all instructions channeled   ___   ___   ___ <br> through a precisely defined organizational structure?

   Or are they given directly to   ___   ___   ___ <br> those selected to achieve them?

	Yes	No	Why?

2. Are committees named only for specific purposes and kept small?

Do they meet promptly at regular intervals, with additional meetings only as required?

3. Does each major department head hold staff meetings at least once in three weeks?

4. Are all decisions involving more than one person or more than one division or department the result of consultation with all necessary persons?

5. Are adequate notes kept of all group discussions and decisions?

Are they issued to all appropriate participants?

6. Does every executive give full consideration to the ideas of his superiors, peers, and subordinates?

7. Are the ideas of all employees freely exchanged for the over-all benefit of the company?

	Yes	*No*	*Why?*
Is there a suggestion or profit improvement plan?	____	____	____

8. Does every executive have, at all times, a clear understanding and a complete listing of the company's general and specific objectives and policies, as well as the objectives and policies which apply to his own division or department? ____ ____ ____

9. Does every executive prepare a list of his duties and responsibilities for his superior and require similar lists from those reporting to him? ____ ____ ____

Do both he and his subordinates know the results required of them? ____ ____ ____

10. Are simple, clear, written instructions given where feasible? ____ ____ ____

11. Has every supervisor learned to organize and schedule his work? ____ ____ ____

12. Does every executive put the company's welfare above his own immediate personal interests? ____ ____ ____

	Yes	No	Why?

How does he manifest this?

13. Does every executive carefully choose and thoroughly train a competent understudy? ____ ____ ____

14. Does every executive delegate authority to his subordinates, place responsibility upon them, and define their accountability for results wherever possible? ____ ____ ____

15. Does every executive deliberately arrange to provide himself with ample time for thought, study, and profitable planning for the future? ____ ____ ____

16. Does every executive encourage his subordinates to develop initiative and use their own judgment to the greatest practical degree? ____ ____ ____

17. Are subordinates so competent that it is unnecessary, and hence undesirable, for their superiors to check anything but end results? ____ ____ ____

18. Are individuals' accomplishments recognized? ____ ____ ____

	Yes	No	Why?

19. Are new positions filled and promotions made from within wherever possible?

20. Are promotions made in accordance with ability, loyalty, cooperation, and total contribution to the company?

21. Is there continuous analysis by division and departments heads to eliminate unnecessary functions, jobs, procedures, paperwork, reports, and duplication of effort?

22. Are all established procedures carefully audited by division and department heads at stated intervals to prevent deterioration or lapse?

Are they periodically re-examined for improvement?

23. Are the company's policies, aims, and plans explained to all executives and supervisors?

24. Are there oversensitive "prima donnas," "big wheels," agitators, parasites?

How are they manifested?

	Yes	*No*	*Why?*

25. Are there incentives for every employee? (This includes department heads and all sub-executives, as well as technical and clerical personnel.) ____ ____ ____

26. Do sound methods of performance measurement exist? ____ ____ ____

Is the performance of every employee appraised periodically? Is there individual counseling with a view to merit increases (according to schedules adopted by the company) or upgrading whenever appropriate? ____ ____ ____

27. Do executives and other employees speak often and with pride of the company's products and methods, where praise is merited, to increase the company's reputation? ____ ____ ____

28. Is the company a stimulating and electrifying place to work? ____ ____ ____

Boil down the essence of the business into one or two statements. State the one key concept that defines the reason for its existence — the service or product, provided to the customer, which he *willingly pays for*.

EXHIBIT B

COMPANY PHILOSOPHY AND BELIEFS

(*Sample Statement*)

The most important task of any business is the blending of human minds so that they will function together effectively. The result is the sort of spirit which distinguishes the good company from the excellent company. Ours is a company which will not be content with less than excellence in everything we do. In order to achieve this excellence, we must develop the habit of strong, positive thinking; and such thinking is developed by knowing what we are *for*, not by knowing what we are *against*.

Our beliefs, the bases for all company policies, therefore follow:

1. The motive power of our society always has and always must come from the tradition of freedom which we have inherited. Thus all external and in-

ternal company transactions will be guided by the four facets of our free enterprise system:

   a. Freedom of economic enterprise.

   b. Freedom of political enterprise.

   c. Freedom of social enterprise.

   d. Freedom of spiritual enterprise.

2. There should be, and can be, perfect unity among the Ten Commandments (or the Constitution of the United States) and our own daily practices as business managers.

3. Sacrificing individual liberty for collective "security" never has produced real happiness. This is as true in the world of business as it is in our life as a nation.

4. Profit is a valid, respectable motive so long as it represents a measure of the company's success in providing society with a useful or desirable product or service.

5. To savor life a man must work hard toward real accomplishment. Unused iron grows rusty; stagnant water becomes murky.

6. Hard, honest work has a distinct value in and of itself.

7. All people work better and achieve more through deep personal faith and confidence.

8. The cultivation of self-discipline is essential to sound human endeavor.

9. No man can truly be successful until he first knows himself. If he lacks the courage to itemize his debits

and credits, he is too often inhibited and handicapped by imaginary shortcomings.

10. Self-interest is normal and natural, but full realization of one's potential can be achieved only through concern for others.

11. We all have strengths and weaknesses, but concentration on increasing the strengths will usually correct the weaknesses.

12. Human needs are better met by giving than by receiving. The value of a company's product or service must outweigh the profit it earns.

13. True satisfaction comes only from giving of one's knowledge and faith, of encouragement, of guidance and constructive criticism — even of material things if need be.

14. Over the long pull it is impossible to give away more than you receive.

15. All human beings have an innate dignity which it must be our aim to preserve in all life's relationships.

16. Untapped potential lies dormant in every man and woman.

17. One of the most thrilling experiences in life is to turn out superior products or provide superior services, and contribute to the overall economy, by working to help common people become uncommonly effective.

18. A sense of proportion — and of humor — is a precious asset in all human relationships, in business and out.

19. Complete integrity is essential at all times to success in working with and through others.

20. The simplest ideas and strategies are generally the best. When we settle for a complex solution to any problem, we have settled for second best.

21. The ideal company climate (practices, attitudes, procedures) is intended to leave each individual free to exercise his talents and skills to the fullest. This, however, he can do only by working hard and wisely toward recognized goals.

22. The person who is a positive thinker and worker will almost always achieve his goals more rapidly than his negative counterpart.

23. Education is not a destination but a continuing journey. Thus the wise man looks forward to learning and developing throughout his business career and his life as a whole.

24. Employees and managers alike should expect to be appraised on the basis of actual results. In no instance will financial compensation or promotion be based upon activity or "busyness" only.

25. The only reason for any of us being on the payroll is to make all our work contribute directly to the objectives of our company.

EXHIBIT C

PROCEDURE FOR REVIEWING OBJECTIVES AND STRATEGIES

Objectives

I. COMPANY

    A. Each department or division head should review the present five-year objectives of the company and submit to the president:

        1. Suggestions for improving or modifying these objectives.

        2. Specific objectives the company should achieve during the next 12 months.

    B. Using the above information, the president will modify the five-year objectives as appropriate and develop the specific objectives he believes the company should achieve during the next year.

II. DEPARTMENT/DIVISION

    A. Each department and division manager will develop the specific objectives that he feels must be achieved in his department to enable the company to meet its objectives for the coming year.

    B. This can best be achieved by:

        1. Listing the things he wants to accomplish during the year.

2. Listing the major problems he would like to overcome.

3. Listing all the opportunities he would like to take advantage of.

4. Taking each of the items on these lists and phrasing it as an objective.

5. Evaluating each of these objectives in light of their practicability, importance to company objectives, and contribution to profit.

6. Listing the objectives in the order of their importance.

7. Determining which ones can be and should be accomplished this year.

C. The manager will then review the resulting list of objectives with the president.

NOTE: The correct statement of an objective is the first step toward attaining it.

Strategic Planning

I. DEPARTMENT/DIVISION

A. Each department and division manager will take one objective at a time and list the things that must be done to accomplish it. That is, he will —

1. List all practical alternatives.

2. Choose the best approach.

3. Arrange this approach in a logical sequence of steps to be followed.

B. The manager will next outline how each of these steps will be accomplished. If necessary, he will follow the procedure spelled out under "A" above.

C. The manager will determine the resource requirements necessary to carry out each objective. He will —
   1. Set up a planning worksheet for each objective.
   2. List each step on the worksheet and determine to the best of his ability:
      a. Personnel, financial, equipment, material, facility, policy, and procedural requirements.
      b. Assignment of responsibility.
      c. Target dates.

D. The manager will determine the coordination with other departments necessary to carry out his plan. This will require him to —
   1. Review the planning steps for each objective and list the information or action needed from other departments to insure successful accomplishment.
   2. List the information that other departments will have to receive from his group to keep well informed.

E. The manager will discuss the information and assistance he needs from other departments with each chief concerned, outlining his specific requirements and fully explaining the reasons for them.

F. The manager will modify his objectives and plans to take into account the needs of other departments.

G. Finally, he will submit his plans to the president for approval.

II. PRESIDENT

A. The president will review, reconcile, consolidate, and approve the plans of the department and division managers.

B. He will incorporate all these plans into a master plan book and use this as a control and a measure of individual performance.

C. He will hold a meeting at which each department head will present his department objectives, with a brief outline of how he plans to meet them, to all the other department heads.

> NOTE: The approved master plan will guide management day by day and week by week. It will be periodically reviewed in light of changing conditions that signal the need for modification.
>
> A beautifully conceived system of plans must only *help* — it must never be a substitute for — daily ingenuity, integrity, discipline, and judgment.

103

EXHIBIT D

SIMPLIFIED AND CONDENSED FORMAT FOR AN
EXECUTIVE POSITION DESCRIPTION

POSITION TITLE:

REPORTS TO:

GENERAL FUNCTION:

RESULTS REQUIRED: ACTION:

METHODS OF MEASURING
RESULTS ACCOMPLISHED:

RESULTS COMMITMENT: 19___

COORDINATION REQUIRED

PROVIDES FOR (functional title)

REQUIRES FROM (functional title)

STATEMENT OF ACCOUNTABILITY

EXHIBIT E

AN INTEGRATED PROGRESS-REPORTING SYSTEM

Basic Requirements

1. The number of reports and the number of recipients should be sharply restricted. Both lists should be scrutinized periodically to determine whether a particular item might not be dispensed with or its distribution curtailed.

2. All necessary reports should be carefully designed to meet the particular needs which they are supposed to fill.

3. Reports should contain only the amount of detail required to serve their purpose and no more; there is a place for the terse, streamlined report, limited to the salient facts or figures, as well as the exhaustive, full-treatment analysis. Generally, the higher the recipient, the less detail is called for.

4. Reports should be timely; that is, they should be issued in time for the management action they indicate to be fully effective. Electronic data processing can be of enormous help here if it is used as a *servant* rather than viewed as a master.

5. Reports should be clear, complete, and accurate, and they should be submitted to the recipients *promptly* when due.

6. Meetings, both regular and special, should be held to discuss progress as reported to date; to coordinate the thinking of functional areas and maintain the best balance among them; and to take advantage of collective judgment.

7. Full supporting data should be available at all times for greater insight in decision making.

Types of Reports Needed

1. Commitments by department, division, company (deviations; actual versus commitments).

2. Budget estimates by department, division, company (deviations; actual versus objectives).

3. Profit and loss statements for overall company and by areas (deviations; actual versus commitments).

Scheduled Reports

1. Financial (general and special):
   a. Profit and loss.
   b. Budget estimates.
   c. Cost reports on all functions.
   d. Others as needed.

2. Production:
   a. Machine capacity (usage).
   b. Cost variables (overtime, etc.).

    c. Scheduling.

    d. Scrap (salvage).

    e. Others as needed.

3. Marketing:

    a. Sales (by product; by product line).

    b. Sales costs (by product, by product line, by type of sales, etc.).

    c. Net profits (by product; by product line).

    d. Research costs.

    e. Research results.

    f. Others as needed.

4. Innovation:

    a. New ideas generated (by function area).

    b. Diversification.

    c. Others as needed.

5. Administration:

    a. Reduced costs.

    b. Increased efficiency.

    c. Conversion of systems.

    d. Others as needed.

6. Personnel:

    a. Employee turnover.

    b. Labor problems.

    c. Training programs.

    d. Morale.

    e. Others as needed.